SUCCESS: MYSTERY TO MATH FORMULA

SIMPLE EQUATIONS TO BUILD YOUR BUSINESS

KARLEEN ANDRESEN

ISBN- 13: 978-0692445259

Published by Kcommons Publishing 2015

DEDICATION

Coming to something like a book doesn't come through a single path nor a fork in the road. It comes by way of many unknown slivers and chasms filled to the brim. Both high and low, I have faced a giant, and been cradled by learning. It is with depth that I share this moment with the highlights of my experience.

Donald, May you know my deepest and most intimate gratitude is reserved solely for you. We have faced demons and you have championed my liberty. May the heavens grant you the greatest and grandest of all the blessings it holds. There is no other who deserves it more. You feed the private chambers of my heart.

My children, You are so near to my heart I can scarcely share my thoughts. I truly thank you and love you: DJ, Anderson, Shaileen, Morgan, and Evaleen. To the others, may you know I wait for you. You are loved. You feed my hope.

Suzanne, May there be a time that I contribute to your professional life in a fraction of the way you've contributed to mine. You feed my business acumen.

Larry, Thank you for the greatest personal counsel at a critical barrier moment, "What problem are you solving…then nothing else matters." You feed my logic.

Neil, You were my first example of entrepreneurship and I so appreciate the continued and generous extension of the olive branch. You feed by spirit.

This is the team of grandeur.

"It could be that it's not plugged in, but that would be too easy."

CONTENTS

"We made $30,000 more last year and it only cost us $60,000."

HOW TO USE THIS BOOK

The first four chapters are the formulas for the business owner specifically. If you're looking at partnership, bringing someone new into the organization, or confirming your own position, use the first four chapters.

Chapters five through ten are the equations to help business, and although there are many other elements, like a business plan, marketing plan, and budgets, these are the fundamentals that will support a strong base for a successful business.

Chapter eleven (no pun intended) is just bonus, icing on the cake. I know small business owners are likely to learn by trial and error because they tend to jump in head first, and think second. This chapter is a kind of safety net of real numbers, a super thinking section.

"My last comment 'appeared' to be inviting feedback. Do not be fooled."

PREFACE

This is it! It's the black book for your small business, and it's set up for what's important to you. The what works approach. Simple to read, understand, and apply; it's about formulas.

Formulas are everywhere. Some are equations like two plus two equals four, a seating grid for a stadium, or counting 20 dollar bills. Other formulas seem to hide in the corner like asking a girl out, plus her acceptance, equals a possible future. A more complex one could be multiple conversations across several networking meetings may lead to a sponsorship for a conference. Even more remote formulas can be found in something like, wanting to help someone, then adding and subtracting many ideas, multiplied by several attempts, results in someone creating a product like a wireless mouse. Building a successful business is more than writing the best code, talking with enough people, or pricing your product, it's all of them. Success does not have a single equation, but it's every equation, the visible and invisible, the obvious and not so obvious. So why the mystery?

Two men asked a group of us how we deal with trials or challenges. There was no mystery for me. My response was quick, "I don't deal with challenges. I deal with choices." That single comment turned into an hour long conversation, and I almost felt like a preacher. Comedian, Kevin Hart, describes the life of an entrepreneur when he said, "...all day, just me, by myself, on the block, holdin' it down..." Although, his routine has nothing to do with business ownership, it's a perfect summary of their life. No matter where you are, or when you start to grow a business, it's one or two players dreaming of something others may not believe they can do. That's the initial business plan in it's entirety. As time progresses, challenges come, and when they do entrepreneurs begin looking for the hidden equations. Some find them, most do not. When it looks like the business is losing the battle, exceptional entrepreneurs will begin scouring for the remote outcomes, or the path less traveled. Statistics tell us successful business owners are rare, only 20 percent or less succeed past their first three years. If we were animals, we would be listed on the critically endangered species list. So if it's formulas, what's the mystery? Why do so few achieve?

Starting a business is basic math. Fill out a business license, pay a fee, open a checking account, and you're open for business. Growing a business are formulas compiled in different ways. Achievement in business is pushing and pulling equations from a remote place. The reason it has been hard is because business owners are looking for the mystery. They're looking to find a needle in a haystack when the formulas are right in front of them. For example, when a challenge hits, even several challenges, most business owners quit. That's basic math. What would happen if instead, the owner considered their challenges as a choice to use a different equation? The first equation or piece would be simple math: I have a challenge. The second part, what are my choices, is the next part of the equation. If you put those together it creates a formula that says, there will be trials and challenges, so... now what? Or

$$\text{Challenges} + (\text{Choices} * \text{How many choices}) = \text{Endurance}$$
$$\text{Endurance} * \text{Repetition} = \text{Success.}$$

Do you see it? In any situation you have two paths: stop or go; do or don't; go forward or move back; succeed or fail. Once that is understood and accepted, like two plus two, the next step is to move on to the next formula. If you decide to press on, then it will be the formulas, how you piece the simple equations together that build success. This is not an isolated rule reserved for the other guy. It's not something that should be ignored.

In seeing more than 3,000 business owners come through my doors, it has been emotional as I've watched most of them fail and fail to listen. This book is being written now, by me, because as singer, Katy Perry, poetically sings, "I used to bite my tongue and hold my breathe, scared to rock the boat and make a mess. So I sat quietly, agreed politely….I've had enough….I see it now. I've got the eye of the tiger…" This book removes the mystery and gives small business owners the formulas they are looking for. Once you read the literal math equations and achievement formulas, the mystery will be gone. You will know if business is made for you. If you feel you have been bitten in the butt with challenge or quandary or you are ready to stop running on the hamster wheel, this book is for you. It is not for the reader looking for legal or accounting advise or the business owner who thrives in trying to be the exception to the rule. With genuine and unbiased affection, business owners looking for a big and bigger life will buy this book. Adopting these formulas will give you more money, more personal satisfaction, and more satisfying relationships that lead to greater ventures and ad-ventures.

The Ultimate Formula

What you will learn in this book:
$$\frac{(K+Y)\,R}{T} = S$$

K = Knowledge
Y = You, your soul, your passion
R = Resistance, barriers, stalls, road blocks
T = Time
S = Success

More than 75 percent
of small businesses will fold
within their first years,
and it will be their hearts that fail them.
Karleen Andresen

1 HEART MATH

Watching a documentary titled *Out of the Clear Blue Sky,* directed by
Danielle Gardner, my thoughts were pushed to question my own
breaking point. With seven children, a caregiver to a husband who
suffered a brain injury more than 20 years ago, and running my own
business, I thought I was resourceful, resilient, and without weakness
in the face of crisis. However, in a riveting 107 minutes that
documentary showed a fortitude that extends beyond reason, and I
found myself longing to know if my heart was made of such
precious metal. This is the first of the leading equations. What is your
heart math formula in business?

9/11 branded America with a memory that created an
unwavering connection. Following the epic hate crime on American
soil, we did not argue about how we felt about terrorism because the
line between right and wrong became instinctively clear. Void of bias
and debate, the political aisle became invisible. All clashing of
cultures vanished, and any separation of status was replaced with
allegiance. Those victims were our victims, our people, and the weeks
that followed were action plans of a united people. Mountains were

literally scaled and people revived. Many opened up their wallets, others made the trek to Ground Zero to help in the weeks that followed. There were prayer vigils and numerous letters to victims' families. That is the heart of the Nation. That is what we did when the panic button was pushed. America united on 9/11, and we remember where we were that morning when the media airwaves lit up with an announcement that changed us. What will happen when a stampede tramples your work?

For the 40-year old Howard Lutnick, CEO and Chairman of Cantor Fitzgerald, 9/11 would find him beyond the edge. His cut throat business approach would become more than industry fodder originally used by his competitors and the board room. In the immediate wake, he becomes the media face of despair for 9/11 and business resilience in its aftermath. He is at the helm of Cantor Fitzgerald beginning in 1991. Before that he was always somewhere within Cantor, cutting his teeth and carving opportunity since graduating from Haverford College. However, September 11, 2001 was to be his Mount Everest. It wasn't a day like most Americans, where he sat polarized in front of the television. He wasn't watching what was happening to other people's lives and then feeling deep compassion and making large donations of time or money. On that day Lutnick stared doom, decimation, and the devil square in the eye. It's the day the clock stopped for the world but began ticking on the most pivotal 48-hours of his business and personal history. Lutnick will rise from below the ashes much like Presidents Washington and Lincoln.

George Washington was the first President of the United States, and as the leader of our Nation, everything he did was uniquely his. He had no previous guidance, no leader to turn to, and every choice set the precedence. His decisions carved paths for future leaders to follow. Washington was an aspiration. Likewise, Lincoln abolished slavery forging a path that had not been traveled. He went against the comforts of his friends and foes, willing to stand as the window to evil until wisdom could find its way to the surface. Both men looked adversity in the eye and dared to consider a Union against compliance. Their heart math equaled fierce resilience that, during 9/11, Lutnick would need to access as well. All three men were faced with considerations which led to enormous obstacles - or opportunities. All three would begin the path emotionally tormented, judged harshly, and still arrive on the other side shredding old traditions and innovating new ones. For the good of their people, each created his own legacy. In Lutnick's case, a modern day business brass, he will work against the odds to cheat death, lose his brother, Gary, in the attack, and rebuild a multibillion dollar operation in two days. In the face of the worst challenge, your power of will is your only asset.

Cantor, as it is abbreviated for insiders, is a financial firm, a Wall Street power player known for their electronic bond trading. According to its website, "Cantor has continued to set the pace in innovation to become a premier global financial services firm….investment bank, recognized for its strength in the equity and fixed income capital markets….Cantor consistently fueled the growth of original ideas, pioneered new markets and provided superior service…offices in over 30 locations around the world…" In the absence of more detail, we get that Cantor is a big deal when it comes to global money flow. The prestigious company headquarters were located on the top five floors of the World Trade Center, North Tower. By all standards, Cantor had arrived and, by its domination, had no plans of releasing its grip on the American dream. At 8 a.m. Eastern Time on 9/11, Cantor literally sat above the clouds on top of the world, and two hours later was ruble and ashes. What came next was harrowing, but outlines the heart equation for success. It's our first lesson of formulas.

This is the first piece of the simple equations. Lutnick had a horrific situation. In a single day, Cantor had just suffered the largest loss of any organization in a single event on American soil. Their 658 losses of life decimated families and silenced Cantor's ability to operate any sensible business, let alone financially service the more than 7,000 institutional clients. He was faced with an imminent choice, and it was going to come with or without his literal participation. The challenge was the unfathomable terrorist attack and its aftermath. The choice was he could build, cut, or bust. In that event, there isn't a human being on the planet that would expect him to open shop as usual in the days following 9/11. The American people had given a worthy pass to everyone directly involved and leniency to anyone wanting to help. But somewhere in there Lutnick surrounded his thoughts and opened business 48-hours later. And in the documentary, you hear the choices become very clear.

It wasn't a simple decision to cut your losses and restructure to open on the public trading market while the Nation mourned. At 8:30 a.m. on September 12, 2011, all the world's bond market leaders came together for their routine conference call and assumed business as usual. No time was taken on that call to rally support and little to no offers of condolences. On the call, the decision was made: the markets would open tomorrow. That's 48 hours after two colossal cement towers came crumbling down claiming thousands of lives. Competitors were ready to make feast on what Lutnick couldn't provide. However, he still had his leader in London and a couple hundred or so other leaders and staff who were not in the World Trade Center at the time. Strategizing was immediate. If Cantor did not open, they would lose everything. The surviving leaders restructured. They trained the London staff on the American markets, they hired pencil pushers to help process orders, and they technically rewired their network to open on schedule. In order to service Cantor clients, Lutnick applied for a loan from JP Morgan Chase in the amount of 70 billion dollars. With his back against the wall, he signed the worst business contract and received the loan. Chase's caveat: we own Cantor if Lutnick and his remaining staff do not demonstrate they have control of the firm…in seven days. It's almost like you can see the vultures circling. I don't fault them. It's business and all sides were doing what investors would expect: pounce when you see a weakness and do all you can for your own company. However, in less than 48-hours Lutnick mourned his own family loss, comforted the Cantor families, mobilized the creation of a crisis center at Ground Zero, dealt with the massive losses for the business, and rebuilt. This was the revised business plan if he wanted a shot at surviving. On September 13, 2011, Cantor opened for business and they were on the trading floor well before others. It is not the event or the trial; it is the choices when the stakes seem burnt to the ground. In Lutnick's case, there is no mystery; it was a formula of his heart, and that's what knowing your heart math does. After the week, he returned to JP Morgan Chase to account, literally. To the Cantor family's outstanding credit, they met the terms of the loan and ownership was returned to its rightful hands. That was pioneering, but Lutnick did not feel his work was finished. His heart had more work. In the immediate days following 9/11, he is seen on the major televisions stations, what seems completely broken, and making the following statement, "It's gonna be a different kind of drive than I've ever had before....There's only one reason to be in business, it's because we have to make our company be able to take care of my 700 families. 700 families. I have 700 families." After the return of Cantor Fitzgerald into his hands, Lutnick opened even wider. In a normal situation of death, families would receive a flower arrangement and condolences at the very best. In Cantor's situation, they established a relief fund for the families. Not only that, but healthcare benefits would be pledged to the families for ten years after the event. A memorial was held for the approximately 5,000 Cantor extended family members, and they've held a memorial each year since. Cantor distributed 25 percent of the company profits for five years following 9/11 and another 45 million dollars in bonuses. Since then, on 9/11 each year, Cantor donates a portion of their profits to the Cantor Fitzgerald Relief Fund in support of the families. It boggles the mind to consider all the obvious and not so obvious loose ends that were taken care of during this crisis, and it was done at the worst of times.

No one would have faulted Howard Lutnick for closing the doors for a period of time. The world expected it. Yet, he stepped up, he leaned into it, and he did something most people would not, and that has created astounding success. The first formula for all great business success stories come by way of challenge. When faced with odds, what will be your story of resilience? What will be your defining moment of greatness, and what will get in your way? You are not let off the hook as an owner. There will be family illness, you may lose face in your industry, someone will discredit or deceive you, your spouse may not be supportive, competitors may pounce, you may be too arrogant, enemies will surface, or many other reasons to falter will show up. What will your heart tell you to do? How deep are you committed to your professional success? Only you know, but considering this ahead of D-day will lend a great comfort in the moment.

Be fair to yourself and your business, and ask yourself the following questions using Lutnick's example and the barriers as a basis:

1. What am I willing to do to ensure success?

_____

_____

2. How deep is my commitment?

_____

_____

3. Why am I in business?

_____

People want to be motivated
More than they want to be educated
Karleen Andresen

2 EDUCATION EQUATION

If you sink your teeth into this equation - without excuses and bias - you will come wildly closer to true success. True success is duplicatable. It's like the power of the franchise. Franchises are a template operation that can be handed to another person and run the same as the first and every subsequent person afterwards can repeat the operation. In business ownership, it's something that can be repeated if you should lose everything or completely change tracks. It comes from the grey matter between your ears. This is the piece that will shift business from a chance with lady luck to a strategic path that is repeatable. It's known by Mark Zuckerberg, Steve Jobs, and Arianna Huffington. The barrier for most small business is resistance thinking. They think they arrived when they merely walked a mile. And while that may be good for the majority, it's not good enough for the great. The key is accepting that learning begins anywhere and never quits. Some people argue when they lack a degree, and it happens with great zest. They feel those with degrees get preferential treatment when they did not earn it with experience. Don't fight a topic that has nothing to do with a piece of paper. People without formal degrees feel devalued when compared to those with degrees. That's a private issue about how time is spent, but it can be easily overcome by shifting to believe in continued learning. On the other hand those with degrees can be found believing they should jump to the top of the heap because they went to college. An appropriate response to this comes through a Human Resource officer of a large organization. She said, "Having a degree is your port of entry, not your right of passage." The most powerful story of education brought me to a man I met back in 1993.

Neil Cannon and I met when he was a client. I was a personal concierge. I organized evenings, weekends, and events for CEOs and top tier executives. They are busy people and I knew they could use a hand in organizing the important but often underserved areas of their lives. In a concierge company the currency you offer is vision, prolific organization, and unbridled resourcefulness. I did not know much about Neil in the beginning, but I was open to learn: rule one, be open to learning in any way, shape, or form it comes in. What came to the surface since we met is Neil is fierce in his business focus. This became obvious when I realized while he was extremely busy doing things like flying to one of his many worldwide offices, and I would receive random envelopes in the mail. Inside would be torn out business articles or other business materials. There would be a sticky note with a personal note from Neil. He had been so impressed with my service and wanted to see me succeed that he was focused on keeping me inside the business loop in spite of how busy he was. He is also clear and uncluttered on the topics most business owners wrestle with. Many owners consume their world with issues that could be decided once and then be a closed topic. Like what to do in a crisis, what to do about the potential of failure, how to view competition, or how successful is successful enough. Since then Neil has become a friend, and I know this because when I call, he calls me back. He shares his expertise when I ask, and he never has a stopping point with me. We are friends because when you take learning and opportunity and mix them together the universe and heaven send you the right people. When the equation presents itself, if you are wise, you honor the opportunity to learn, and you are educated by your business superheroes.

Neil is one of my entrepreneurial superheroes. He has traveled an education path that anyone else can do. He began business with no higher education. He took what he had, natural strategy and instinct, and let that work for him. He and his partner built a grand business that has impacted every person with a department store credit card in their wallet right now. Later, he decides on a formal education and even expands that to another industry altogether. Traditional or unorthodox, quantity is not the name of his game, it's quality of his natural self and quality of his choices. His timeline goes from starting a business, learning on the fly, being curious enough to ask, and learning on the job, which many business owners do. Later Neil enters a business program through Harvard and earns his degree. Where most stop, Neil forges on and earns his doctorate to enter a completely different industry. He never lets go of his thirst for education. That is one of the primary keys to his enormous success.

His first round is motivation. Neil is strolling through life just fine. He's not making world impact, but he's a responsible contributor to society and nothing horrible is looming over his head. He's reading through a local newspaper and sees an ad that calls out to him. It's a speaking conference with none other than the motivational and iconic Zig Ziglar. Zig is speaking on attracting a bright future, and Neil bites on the opportunity which will become a moniker for his success. After attending the one day conference, he is so moved that Neil says, "It all made sense. I made the decision [for success], and I've never looked back."

Schmidt-Cannon International later became Aspen Marketing. It's a sobering story. Two teenagers, Joe Schmidt and Neil Cannon, sold inexpensive gold necklaces and assorted jewelry at the local swap meet each Saturday morning. They began their mega-business with a thousand dollars. Joe and Neil would get to the swap meet early to find the best spot. and they dedicated to remain all day. According to Neil, Joe is incredibly likable and, "…people would buy from someone they liked." Of course Neil dealt with people too, but he was geared more toward the business side, the strategic focus. Both were hard workers and brought their best to their business. The spontaneous education would become the seeding of history.

Leveraging a positive relationship Joe had with a Sears® store manager, Frank Vasquez, the partners gained entry to sell their jewelry in Sears. "It's what happens when you're likable," he said, and they moved their swap meet business into Sears. Then, as Neil tells it, he and Joe went to lunch with Mark Charvat, the customer service manager. In a seemingly unimportant moment, Mark told them he was having a difficult time getting people to sign up for the Sears credit card. He explained his job success at Sears included his success with credit card applications. It didn't stop there. Like many businesses, his performance reviews were also based on completed applications. To grasp the context, in those days, every credit card holder was worth 500 dollars or more in incremental revenue to the company. For retailers, the credit card holder brought great value, and what Mark, Joe, Neil, and the economy were unaware of, is all were about to change and make history. During this pivotal lunch Mark mentioned he had a budget for his program. As if the heavens opened and the angels began to sing, Joe and Neil swapped glances and realized the opportunity of a lifetime had dropped like mana from heaven. The dynamic duo knew this nibble had potential. They left and came back a few days later with the perfect idea; their plan for success. For every completed credit card application, the applicant would receive a free gold necklace. This was a time void of the Internet and when identity theft was a conspiracy concept; so logistically it was a free gold necklace for filling out a piece of paper. Sears would buy the necklaces as part of the spending budget, and Joe and Neil would hand them out and garner completed applications. A friendly lunch, an innovative idea of transferring how to use the hours, and taking your hands off the wheel is an educational moment for small business owners today. Mark liked the idea and with their hard working passion, the duo went a step farther to go big or go home. The two young men made large displays and signs which were unheard of in that day. Then the launch; that day of reckoning. In the first weekend, it was the best promotion ever run. This grand success found wings. With Mark's help, the two became educated in the Sears organization and who to talk to. They made their presentation and within months Sears invited Schmidt-Cannon to use the same promotion strategy in their Los Angeles district of 25 stores. Three month later they expanded into the Sears Western Region of another 200 stores, and before the end of the year they were managing Sears nationally along with JC Penney® nationally and the former Montgomery Wards® nationally. Of course, over time, products changed to include other things like summer trinkets, bottles of soda, and yes, gold necklaces. Schmidt-Cannon was at the root of this movement. Before this, there were some universal cards like Diners Club® and BankAmericard®, but department stores had not found their spotlight until now the innovative ideas brewed in the minds of two young men. The department store credit card impact has trickled down to the consumer as well. These business card sized plastic cards have been instrumental in helping individuals establish credit. That credit has assisted millions in their ability to qualify for car purchases, home buying, and securing personal loans and business loans. To see the business rewards, when Neil retired from Aspen Marketing in 2002, it was a quarter of a billion dollars, and they serviced top companies, and still retained the top 25 of the top 26 retail department stores in the United States. The early work shifted the economy and Joe Schmidt and Neil Cannon stand as tremendous educators of business success. These are the stories entrepreneurs feed on. It moves us, but will we learn from it? It doesn't stop there, the remaining education trail continues towards a chasm of learning.

I received a one way ticket on the learning locomotive that

would take me from curious to humble pie in a single conversation. "I'm thinking about continuing my education to get my Master's degree..." I probed during a phone call with Neil. "Why do you want a Masters?" Because I want my education to open doors. His response was pointed yet peaceful, "By the time you get out of school the information will be outdated. You could spend the same money attending quality seminars and conferences and have current and relevant information." I pushed back, "But, Neil, you have a degree from Harvard. You have a large company. People will listen to you just because you speak, and I want that." Wait for it..., "Karleen, I didn't get my degree until I was a 10 million dollar company." What!? Ouch! Neil Cannon and his partner, Joe, grew their company from one thousand dollars to ten million before Neil went to college! He was attending what many would say is the school of hard knocks. That was a learning moment no university could have given me. Those words reverberated off the walls of my office., "...[not] until I was a 10 million dollar company." I swallowed the lump in my throat, and sat back in my chair. I was being taught at the feet of my appointed mentor. I learn something each time I speak with him: from a self inflicted reality check or the recipient of his kindness in sharing his knowledge. Education is found everywhere.

Neil built a quality business that thrives today. He stepped down in 2002 but continued his education equation. He wanted to help the sexually abused. so he earned his Ph.D. in Human Sexuality and his clinical training is in marriage and family therapy. Taking what he learned in the early days and bringing it all the way forward to formal education, Dr Neil Cannon has a thriving business practice, is a Professor and guest lecturer, and mentors a couple dozen other students. He absolutely loves his new journey and felt called to it. This is a exemplary example of the never ending opportunity to learn in every situation and every opportunity, formal and informal.

The next step in the success formula is gaining and being open to quality education. It's seizing moments to leverage and build positive relationships, it's innovation, and it's learning more in each situation. A worst case scenario is for the business owner to think success is total achievement. It is not. When this happens, progress stops, and opportunities will be missed. Quality education comes through many methods like:

- Universities
- Community colleges
- Night classes
- Weekend and week long conferences
- Downloadable but qualified trainings through privately held companies
- Non-credited single courses offered through the local university
- Continuing education courses
- Online education through colleges
- Certification programs
- Finding a mentor
- Local school district community classes
- Local non-profits focused on helping build business

It is your time. The education equation beckons to you like the ad Neil saw in the newspaper. When called to respond, will you say yes or will you have other plans? When opportunity knocks like what happened in the Sears store, will you say yes, or will you say there isn't enough money or enough foot traffic? When being offered training to help maneuver you through the learning system, will you say yes or will you put it off to the never-ending calendar? It's your time, and you get to decide, but here are some questions to help you move forward.

1. Do I believe in continuing my education and through what method, either from something on the list above or another way?

_____

_____

2. What bit of knowledge would I like to learn more about and why?

_____

_____

3. What would learning do for my work and/or life?

_____

_____

Ahhh,
the energy of
a mustard seed
is all you need
Karleen Andresen

3 ZERO BALANCE

Zero balance is the $E=mc^2$ part of success. The law of relativity. I'm sure the idea is confusing already. Think of it this way, there are symbolisms which speakers, writers, and motivators use to inspire others to action; yet, they don't actually know how to use it. For example, motivators may use the idea of multi-tasking to help busy and overwhelmed mothers feel better about what they are doing when, in fact, multi-taking is a myth. Another is you can have a balanced life, when in fact, your life is never in balance. People are giving eight, 10, 14 hours to the job and the rest of the waking hours are being split among family and companion time, volunteer work, and spiritual learning. The law of relativity is another one. It is used as an example of discerning judgement, innovation, and in showing purpose. When you hear speakers use the law of relativity, it automatically makes a person think "brilliant." For the motivator speaking to the layman, that's the purpose. Let's make the listener think it's mind exploding and you, the speaker, gain credibility. How many people really know what it means? $E=mc^2$ means energy equals mass multiplied by the speed of light squared. For the purpose of zero balance, it means the power within (E) equals your body's (m) ability to respond (c) to a situation multiplied. In other words, how you handle having nothing creates your outcome. Mastering this equation means at the worst of times, there is a plan, even if you don't use it. When do you use zero balance? When crisis wields its head, when the absolutely unexpected happens in your world, or when it feels like the world around you has abruptly and unexpectedly ended. Your energy response at the speed of light, squared.

It was four in the morning and all is quiet; a rare moment in a home with two parents bustling with five young children. I'm nine months pregnant with baby number six. We've just moved and we've been frantically cleaning and fixing our home in need of some serious attention. But at this hour I'm standing on the stairs to lessen the foot difference in height between me and my husband, Donald. All is peaceful and the entryway is dark. He's going to be gone for three days; something we did twice a month. His reward for top sales in the company is he gets the brass ring of territories, San Francisco. With my head on his chest I whisper, "Be careful; just be careful." Those are the last words I said before the airport shuttle picked him up. A couple short hours later, the house comes alive. Curtains are being sewn, and children are cleaning grout in the kitchen. At eleven that morning the phone rings. I was standing next to the large French windows looking at the front yard when I heard his voice, "I was in an accident. He blew the stop sign and hit me. Something is wrong. I don't feel right." He hung up and that was all I had to go on. Later I receive a call from the hospital. It's my first link to find out what's happening. The nurse says the doctors want Donald to stay overnight for observation, but he's refusing. She says, "I am calling to let you know that he is leaving, and we cannot legally keep him here if he demands to leave. I don't know what he is going to do, but he is leaving." To this day, he does not know how he got to the airport or on his flight. He said something about a motorcycle, but doesn't remember. Through no fault of his own, this is his third accident in nine months. I pick him up at the airport later that night. His six foot two inch frame balled up in the front seat of our van and he said, "My head feels like it's going to explode. I don't want to see anyone, and I don't want anyone knowing what happened." That began my war cry. I would spend the next 16 years protecting him, guarding him, fighting him, and keeping this a secret from everyone, even our seven children for 14 years.

If there is such a thing as hell on Earth, I was about to take up residence. I gave birth to our sixth baby five days after his accident. As if this was our first round, he was so moved about the miracle of birth. He compared it to having a sports car and was almost giddy about this baby boy. Shortly after the birth, Donald left the hospital and returned with baby gifts hanging off every part of his upper torso. He was thrilled, and I had never seen him this excited about a baby's birth. A week later I shared how touched I was by his reaction. His response, "What? What are you talking about?" It was a shattering moment. He had no recollection. No recollection of the birth, no recall of how he laid his head on a table so he could see eye level through the clear basinet at his baby, and no memory of the gifts he bought. Something was wrong. Unbeknownst to us, the months ahead would be riddled with him frequently running stop signs and stop lights, unable to read signs, forgetting what words mean, not being able to remember where he was on the planet or where I was. He would go to the grocery store two blocks from home and not return for three hours because he lost track of time. He would go to the school to pick up children and come home with with only one or two because he forgot how many children he had. He would pull things out of the oven without hot pads and accidentally put dish towels on open flames on the stovetop because he forgot what hot was or what fire did. One day he watched our young daughter in a neighborhood spa. She slipped off the step and was submerged under water. As her arm was reaching up, eyes bulging, and the bubbles from her body floated to the top of the water, Donald stood there rubbing his head. Sitting out of reach I screamed, "Pull her out!" He did but later said, "I knew something was wrong, but I couldn't figure it out. I didn't know what to do." He was rude to friends who came by because while they treated him as usual, but he didn't remember them and struck back verbally because he felt intruded upon by strangers. Neither of us knew what was happening. I began juggling the excuses on his behalf. From laughing it off, "He was probably teasing!" to "Hmm, I wonder what that's about?" I took the blame, excused him, and offered off-handed replies. I didn't know what was happening, but I was his wife and I stood stalwart in honoring my commitment to him on that first night home. He didn't want to socialize so I began turning down invitations. He had a temper now, which was contrary to what I had known before. He was verbally abusive and during one heated exchange early on he physically charged me like a linebacker. Because of the position I was in, when he charged, my Anterior Cruciate Ligament (ACL) was torn. The stories go on and on with him putting me through a wall, me stepping in between him and our children during any and every one of his rages, and driving around looking for him when he would randomly stop mowing the lawn and walk off. No one could lend us help on understanding what was happening, but it was happening! He was our sole wage earner, and everything was screeching to a halt emotionally, intimately, and financially. People were quick to judge our silence and retreat, which was another layer of conflict I took on the chin. My world, our world completely changed into something I didn't sign up for and nothing we could have anticipated. We went from a Cinderella story to two scared people, and we attacked each other with a vengeance.

I wasn't pure in the situation. I married someone I thought I could depend on as a partner, and that was instantly stripped from me. The layers of security and safety a relationship offers was void, and I resented it. I still kept his secrets and was silent in public. People would never know, but behind the scenes I was impatient, excruciatingly judgmental of his actions, but I grew to be a great and respectable warrior of my family. The kind rivaled only by the great warriors we watch in the movies. My five foot two inch frame had no fear. When Donald would square up against me, my toes would be directly in front of his. At that time my zero balance had conceded that I would die to protect whatever was necessary: my husband against judgement, my children against my husband, and our family's reputation against the world. We lost the confidence of our friends and family, and that was never regained. Donald had constant head pain and would roll around on the floor begging me, "Please get a gun and shoot me. I can't take the pain. Please find a gun. Please." While I was losing the battle with my husband's health, we were losing the battle with the insurance company.

When something like an accident on the job strikes, the insurance company strikes back. There are rules to follow when worker's compensation is involved. You have to get things approved and always ask permission, and then wait. They stop and start the temporary financial benefits in hopes of pushing a person back to work so it limits their liability. They bring in their specialists to ensure there is a counter testimony to the doctors treating the patient. If you fail to make doctors appointments, the insurance company uses that to show lack of dedication and integrity. They can even be found sneaking around your home to videotape the patient doing things like putting clothes in a washer so they can show full functioning ability. Their main goal is to discredit the person in any way. I had to become vigilant in helping Donald get the best and consistent care needed. With all the insurance games, I went back to work and the house fell apart. Everything fell apart. Donald didn't really know who I was, nor did he care. He was disengaged and volatile, but hope would keep me clinging as I would see brief moments where Donald seemed normal.

It would take four years to diagnose Donald with a moderate to severe brain injury. Back in those days, there wasn't the same awareness or sensitivity of head injuries as there is today. It would take another ten years to adjust to an unknown world. He finally told our seven children after 14 years, and so many things began making sense for them, but the circumstances couldn't be changed. Although in public I made sure we appeared as close as a sports team, behind the scenes I kept his secrets and we destroyed out marriage to ruble, to zero.

Our life together has not been simply challenging, it has seen destructive and a complete leveling of two human beings. That's zero balance. In business or life, if you lose everything you worked for, what will you have left? In business success, do you have a plan should you lose everything you think you have? What will you do should you awake to an empty bank account, a fatal diagnosis or accident, or loss of all your staff? When tragedy hits, it is difficult to get a reasonable mind around the situation in that moment, which is why many people fold at that time. If you can verbalize and understand your deepest worries today and then create a plan to respond to it, chances of success would be waiting in the wings.

Zero balance made a shift. For years I was expecting the Donald I knew to return. And when you lose everything, returning to the exact same is not an option. It wasn't a conscience expectation, but when I accepted that my husband died in the accident, and another man came home in his place, everything shifted. Once I realized it was the same body but a different man, I began looking at my relationship differently. It's a moment of reinvention. There were still salvageable pieces even when I thought all was lost. For example, I realized this man did not receive the same respect I would give another. He did not receive minor consideration like asking permission to have friends over. He wasn't a recipient of my kindness, and he wasn't given the option to choose this life that he didn't completely remember. Once I reconciled there were still tools to give, the zero turned upward. I began looking at my options toward success. Being angry when he lost track of time ended because that is what my reaction would have been for other people I knew. Like I did for others, I extended more understanding as he coped with his limitations, I assumed the best of him, and vocalized his good qualities. Another tool, I verbally gave him the option to choose me, on his terms, if at all. When it looked like zero was the balance, there were still options, resources, and possibilities. There were still good directions when it seemed the worst direction was the only direction. Today, Donald is an exquisite and exceptional human being. He always was. I am grateful for the privilege of being called his wife. Regardless of where we go, he will always be a divine and gifted man.

Considering the notion of losing everything is an idea businesses rarely consider; they believe the idea of failure should not be in the business plan. That's a mistake. Even if you lose and recover, the experience of the losing everything changes you. Like my story, take the worst case plight and ask yourself, what do you still have left? $E=mc^2$ is not understood by most because we fail to look at it, we fail to study it and understand how it applies to our life. But it does apply. An article by Joshua Carroll on the Universe Today website, explains the power of the human being in a fun way.

If you apply the $E=mc^2$ formula to your power, Carroll illustrates the human being has more than 88,000 times more energy than the Atomic Bomb that leveled Nagasaki, Japan during World War II! That's not a period, that's an exclamation point! Take that in! You have more power inside your body than something that decimated a city! This is the formula no business giant speaks of, but this is where dreams are leveled or brought back to life. Look at the worst idea toe to toe and determine that you will still have options should that come to pass. You can go rebuild, restructure, and rejuvenate any and every situation especially in business. Get this equation branded into your memory and you will have the formula of success by the tail. Here are some questions to determine your zero balance resistance.

1. What is my worst case scenario, or my #1 fear?

_____

_____

2. If the worst happened, what options, decisions, tools, resources, or ideas will I still be in control of?

_____

_____

3. What is the absolute first benchmark I must reach if I have nothing?

_____

_____

Success isn't chance

It's choice

Karleen Andresen

4 STRATEGIC SUM

An equation where ego trumps income. This is the toughest chapter to write because if you don't say it sensitively enough, business owners kick the idea back as rubbish. The challenge at this moment is how can I say this delicately enough that owners will breathe it in? What's the best approach so owners don't shoot their selves in the foot? And then it hits me. I can't! Formulas don't work that way. You put the information into the light and test it to see where it lands. Because I'm dealing with the tender feelings of the human being, most likely rooted in something other than business, there will be no absolute right approach. So, I'm going to pull off the bandaid, and we're going in.

Ignore this formula and you are destined to be limited. This is what comes between owning a small one or two man operation to a sweltering mega enterprise. Let's be frank, it's where you get in the way of success, even when it's your success. We've heard the idioms, cut off your nose to spite your face, don't bite the hand that feeds you, you're too big for your britches, pride goeth before the fall. That's you in this equation. These idioms reflect the business owner who lets ego get in the way. Why? It's pride, foolishness, and a absence of authentic truth. Think about it this way, if someone came along to give you the answer to happiness, what might you say? Pause before you answer that, which you probably didn't. What would you authentically say? Some years back there was a story being reported. A man was on the streets of a metropolitan city handing out twenty dollar bills. I watched the news. He was extending his hand, smiling, and saying something like, "Here. Here's a gift." A few would take the gift after encouragement from the man. It looked a little like begging, "Please, this is a gift, no strings attached." Sadly most were rejecting it. There were suspicious yet kind rejections, "No, that's okay…No thank you…Thank you, but no." Others would take obvious steps backward from the extended hand. Still others ignored the man completely and kept walking. This is human kind's authentic response to gifted opportunities. We become suspicious. We don't want the help or extended hand of another. Today, there is a YouTube video titled *What If The Homeless Gave You Money* by fouseyTUBE which shows a progressed response to the same idea today. It shows that we think we're better. We can do it on our own. We don't want to appear weak or in need. Somewhere in the dark corners of our thinking, we doubt the obvious. We cast it aside with more passion than we accept things. That is what makes you your own worst enemy here.

When you're given an opportunity and then push against it, that's avoiding the magic in the strategic sum. It's when your mind fails you. You either ignore, kindly disregard, or flagrantly discount opportunities being offered. Nonsensical business owners instinctively operate outside the strategic sum. One year a woman gave a 10 thousand dollar sponsorship to a woman named Shelley. It was her first sponsorship for a conference about changing your life. Shelley was disorganized and lacked enough leadership to put together a sponsor package. The request was declined several times until a mutual and well respected friend requested the sponsorship on her behalf. In the absence of a sponsor package, the sponsor created her own and Shelley gladly accepted it. However, Shelley delivered on only part, the small part, of the package. She used the sponsors's leads, connections, and name and never delivered on the promised package. At the time of restitution the sponsor confronted Shelley about the final obligation. Shelley acting overwhelmed but promised to fulfill her obligation. After the conference she never reconnected and she disconnected from the sponsor who provided the help. The next year, Shelley went to a competitor of the sponsor and partnered with her. There are several lessons to learn. The obvious is Shelley is a poison in the strategic sum. She was not interested in a mutual relationship; she stole respect. She is also one of the reasons companies hesitate to sponsor new groups; the lack of experience to professionally deliver is a deterrent. The final lesson is respect the sum. Burning a bridge in a mutual project is never a good idea.

The reason people poison the sum is because every business owner has star-filled eyes when they step on the stage of ownership. Instead of creating mutual cohesion, they use what politicians and economists call the Potemkin (pronounced pro-tem-kin) Village effect. A fake facade. Potemkin was a close confidant, perhaps a lover of Catherine the Great, ruler of Russia, in the 1700s. Trying to garner support from allies prior to another war, dignitaries were invited to preview the villages Catherine had established since the last war. She was attempting to show her acumen for establishing new colonies along the river front. The story goes that Gregory Potemkin went ahead of the procession and erected impressive, yet mobile, villages for show. He used his own men as village members and once the group observed the villages from a distance, the village would be torn down and moved ahead and re-erected. This became a practice for Potemkin during Catherine's six month journey. A Potemkin Village is a fake village built to impress. It is meant to appear better than things really are. That is what most owners do! That is what Shelley did when she used the mutual friend to garner sponsorship. She offered a facade so it appeared to be wholesome when potential sponsors came by. This is poison to mutual agreements.

The strategic sum is coming together with another person or

organization in a single focus, activity, series of events, or intention. There is a mutual goal and expectations each side would like to see. Strategic alliances usually look like:

- Sponsorships
- Collaborative projects
- Alliances with businesses that compliment yours
- Temporary projects focused on a goal

These literal activities look like trade shows, conferences, networking meetings, online events, auctions, specialty publications, race events, fairs, newsletters, and this list is open to any other intention that can be innovated. But it's when something is organized and others contribute something like money, influence, or both in order to participate.

A few examples are a newsletter offered through HARO whom has more than 100,000 media interested customers. If writers, reporters, editors are your target, for a few hundred dollars HARO is willing to write about three lines endorsing your company. That will go at the beginning of their newsletter. Another is two, three, or ten companies put a flyer together to launch something, and everyone sends the flyer out to their list of contacts. Something a little more difficult for new entrepreneurs to understand is a conference sponsorship. Would you pay 20 to 50 thousand dollars to speak on a stage for an hour? This is what I call pudding. Before you respond with shock at the organization with this kind of expectation, understand that you must have sufficient confidence in what you offer before getting on this stage. Most get confused thinking the cost is the problem. It is the barrier of the business owner that is the conflict. If you have something valuable to offer, then you should be able to sell it. That's the question. Do you have the talent and ability to sell what you offer on stage? If you do, then the formula of questions should be what do you need out of the sponsorship, and writing the check to get on stage. This can generate millions. Another idea is putting on a mutually beneficial event. Partnering with a race, walk, or tournament by offering a packet pickup location can put your business front and center for a health focused audience, a cancer healing group, or a family focused crowd. This is when and where magic happens.

The power of coming together is where enormous growth can take place. Expanded attendance, authority, profit sharing, community leadership, sharing talent sources, sharing information, and the list goes on about the benefits of a healthy partnership. This is highly recommended, but it's a high level form of doing business. Business owners need a vision for this because it can be costly to play and costly to lose. I encourage sponsorships, but use this formula to determine if it's right:

- What am I wanting out of this investment (speaking, leads, exposure, presence, nothing)?
- Is this my target audience?
- Why are they attending? What do the audience members think they will hear about?
- Do I have the skills to capture what I'm wanting from this investment?
- Is this a buying audience?
- How does this event rank against others I have seen?
- If money was no object, would this event still be a good idea?

These additional questions are good but their importance depends on what you need to get out of the experience:

- If I do not recover my investment or more, how will I feel about this sponsorship?
- Will I receive a leads list from this sponsorship?
- Is this a business I want to have next to my name?

Let's face a few facts. You deserve to have everything you put your heart and energy into. But everyone needs a little help from friends, or forget friends, places that create great alliances. Tragically, more often than not, when approaching a potential project partner, a sponsor idea, or a strategic partnership, the mouth waters at the idea of conquering. The idea that a bank might see enough in your project to hand you several thousand dollars almost makes your chest puff up like a peacock. Resist the temptation and focus on mutual value and long term vision of the relationship. To offer great value of your own, ask yourself the following questions:

1. If I sponsor something, what is the one thing I want more than anything else?

_____

_____

2. What three current activities, events or companies have my target audience?

_____

_____

3. What tools or resources do I offer a sponsorship (large list, money, speakers, other potential partners, ticket sales etc)?

_____

_____

I have not failed.
I've just found 10,000 ways
that won't work.

Thomas Edison

5 LIST BUILDING FORMULA

Ahhhh, list building; the Holy Grail of business success. Your list is the source of all good things when you care for it with integrity. When I speak with clients I describe this list as a room of hand selected, premium quality, and gifted human beings. They are the best of the best of your target audience. They are interested, invested, and inquiring people sitting on the edge of their seat waiting for the next announcement. The people in the room feel, found, or sense something magical in you. You are providing them with something that makes them follow you. They have decided to trust you, and I say decided because society by nature is apprehensive. So, yes, they decided to trust you enough to come into your room. They believe in whole or in part that you will provide them with the very best they are seeking. And I will add, if you have decided to be a leader in your field, you should have decided to provide them with the very best you can find. If you are worth your weight in knowledge, you will continually strive to find better expertise and be better in what you provide as well. This quality of leader is not like the 80 percent or more of the people who settle for resources and talents that are easy to get to. S/He does not limit her/his reach to what's local and immediate; they expand because they care that their list gets the best of the best as well.

I was working with a top line speaker, Nathan Ogden. He is a quadriplegic that focuses on providing steps to move from being paralyzed in life and business to being outstandingly productive. It's a very cool story in many different ways, but one of his experiences that lodged in my mind is when a nurse had misgauged his oxygen when he was first injured. There he is, laying helpless and frozen in the hospital. Nothing moved except his eyes. A pretty standard beginning which sounds like a movie. A well intended nurse had miscalculated the amount of oxygen he was to receive through his machine, and she dialed it down to about half of what was needed. Can you image? His mind is fully functional with nothing else but his eyes to communicate, and that is only if someone is looking directly at him and knows how to communicate with the paralyzed. It was evening and very dark in the room. All Nathan could hear were the machines and the voice of borderline panic in his head. He felt himself slowly slipping away: dying. The mental torture; to know you are trapped inside a slowly dying body with a fully functioning mind. While he's nearing mental terror, the world strolls around him like a well timed symphony. He knows people are working, smiling, and walking. He's imagining his family without him, his wife with a new lover, and his children with a new father. It is unbelievable! By his own will, he calmed himself and did what he needed to survive. On a fluke, a nurse came in and realized the mistake and corrected it. Once this happened, a protective allegiance kicked in. Nurses pay special attention, the hospital tracks down how the mistake happened and makes appropriate corrections. His family got a crash course in becoming a voice for Nathan. That is similar to the relationship between a business owner and their list. Your list is your charge. I described the list vision to Nathan and gave him the stewardship to protect and provide for those on his list who trusted him. Then I posed the scenario, how would he respond to allowing anyone in the social media field to present and make a sales offer to his audience? He was still and sober. I could tell he went there in his mind. He responded with questions, "Would they have the experience, the expertise, the success rate to be in front of my audience?" In that moment, Nathan became a leader of his list, and he became more concerned and protective about who would gain access. Building a list means they trust you sufficiently to allow you to make some decisions for them, like who you recommend. When you discount the stewardship you find much of what is out there now, a lot of riffraff.

Most of what I see is a pure pimp and prostitution system: dangle something free out there and see how many take it. Once they bite and dare to steal a piece, a pimp comes along and backs them up against the wall and says, "Pay up!" These people are bottom feeders. They talk sweet, say all the right things, use charm more than knowledge, and speak with a two-edged sword. Then gut you for dollars with no real value. This system is more common than quality care. I have watched individuals and group leaders willing to sell to the highest bidder. Some groups require people to do business with those in the room without ever knowing their qualifications, and thousands upon thousands of dollars are lost in this system. There are others who expect people to give to them citing "reciprocity" or "service" while they apply fees to everything. Still others will take a stance like, if you do not join my group, I will compete with you. Shocking but true, and more common than you might think. Accomplished business owners do not need to be like the majority.

There was a man who led a group of business owners. I approached him about a strategic sum (See Strategic Sum chapter for an explanation). It was a collaborative magazine. My company already had a business magazine and creating a strategic alliance seemed natural and a way I could help a struggling business. He was very interested and asked for details. After showing him the problem, the solution, and the method to success, I offered his business a 50 percent stake in the profit. At his enthusiastic request I drafted the letter to announce the partnership program to both his and my list.

This single project would have resulted in a minimum 20 thousand dollar annual increase to his bottom line; something no one else was offering. In addition, my company was shouldering all the operational time and processing. It seems like a major win, and it was. After he had seen everything and approved the letter, he asked me to wait for a couple weeks before we announced. So I held, and then began the spiral of failed responses to my emails and phone calls. A month later, it hit the fan. He released a copycat magazine using my product format, tag line, and font style. When confronted about the situation he said, "It's purely coincidence," but saw no further need to continue our project. When other people began challenging his integrity, he called me for a meeting. He turned on the charm that seemed to curry favor with others, but I could not shake the reality of his actions. We ended our meeting at a standstill. To his credit, he is a list builder. To his discredit, he fails to honor the list. Interestingly this man's group has had several dozen leadership changes over the three years and he is garnering a declining reputation. There was a issue so significant that his partner pulled out of the business, and his organization cannot seem to cover its costs unless people give it to him for free. Also interesting, the food businesses that house his networking meetings have either closed or reported losing revenue on his audience. So how can you avoid this kind of problem?

Powerful list building is a formula of behavior. I have done it, and I have watched it. It takes caring to build a quality list and then caring for the list. Three great list building organizations are HubSpot, the Suzanne Evans organization, and HowDoesShe. Hubspot is in technology and SAAS business. Suzanne Evans in a coaching organization, and HowDoesShe is an online craft sharing site. The purpose of these organizations beyond their stellar following is to illustrate the formula works in any industry. These groups have nearly a hundred thousand followers to several hundred thousand followers. Building a list like this means converting a percentage of their audiences into higher paying clients or offering programs to allow others to get in front of their audiences. These leaders take care of their list, they listen to and address the conversations happening, and they offer what is relevant for their people. They respect their audience, and in turn their audience respects them, and growth happens. It doesn't just happen. It is work, but when properly acquired, your list is the number one resource. Here are a couple formulas to begin building your list and apply integrity in operating.

Here are a few methods to collect names:
- Collect business cards.
- Participate in a trade show every six months.
- Sponsor a small event with a buying target audience.
- Sponsor a show where you can speak and make an offer.
- Offer to speak for free to smaller groups.
- Use social media to promote your offerings.
- Write for other blogs that speak to your target audience.
- Offer a free day training and make a bold offer at the end.
- Put on a conference with strategic partners and everyone promotes your offering to their list.
- Ask a local store if you could put up a table.
- Become a member of a local association and go down their membership list to expand your own list.

The formula of list building.
- In it's simplest equation, list building is collecting business cards at a networking meeting, trade show, after hours event, or association attendance. You take those cards and put them into your list to make calls, have meet ups, or add them to your email list.
- Go a little deeper to create connection and you'll invite people to your newsletter, a free webinar, to download a white paper, or to watch a video. Unfortunately, owners are undisciplined and inconsistent, which will cause struggle. Distress happens because public response takes

time. List building takes time, and that's part of this formula. At a time when we have become accustom to instant gratification and the overnight sensation stories, being patient is frustrating. Growing a relationship is hard. With a halfhearted effort, this is where most companies start crying "failure" when in fact it is their failure of communicating consistently with their audience. It's a failure to provide worthwhile content in a format they want that is the culprit.

♦ To capture success, the formula goes deeper still. There is a series of behaviors. Yes, you can begin at the lowest level of collecting business cards. However, add invites, webinars, downloads, and videos on a consistent bases. Let these flow into the third leg of small fee workshop, joining with another organization through sponsoring events and programs, offer a series of trainings, or a series of audio interviews. The key to applying these is consistency. Create a schedule of stories, knowledge pieces that are written out, inspirational elements, and content, and you will capture leads. All three list building companies mentioned earlier all operate in this part of the formula, and their emails are frequent and juicy. Becoming a person who provides valued information takes the third part of the formula.

If you're still stuck, begin by asking yourself the following questions and then go back to the two lists above.

1. What do I know that I could write, record, or video tape and then share?

_____

_____

2. Do I have or can I create enough content to offer something every week of the year? If so, get it into an automated system?

_____

_____

3. If I care about what my audience learns, what would I tell them?

_____

_____

I can't imagine a person becoming a success
who doesn't give this game of life
everything he's got.
Walter Cronkite

6 MARKETING PIECES MULTIPLIED

The source of deep heartache for marketers is what business owners do with the marketing pieces. It's called collateral or marketing collateral in the industry. It's because owners use this number one face of their business and discount it into the hands of amateurs. For example, there is a former successful car salesman who retired and now teaches people how to design business cards. What!? My first thought to the business owners is, are you completely insane, do you care about your business at all, are you okay living to the least common denominator? My last thought is, you better be a humdinger of a salesperson so they ignore everything they see or begin planning how to close your doors today. How does a brilliant, level headed, go-get-em business owner buy into this rubbish? It's a formula of decision making: a slick talking salesman swoons an eager business owner to believe he will be a millionaire by using his design. Humph!

Let me see if I can illustrates how impactful branding is. Take a look at the following chart. In the first column are good brands. Reading the list, you may be able to recall those brands with ease and have an instant relationship with it. Associated to those brands are experiences or songs, sounds, colors, or remembering what their overarching message is. That's part of their brand. In the next column, it may trigger the same, but those are brands that were rejected by the public and the last column offers the reason why the poor brand was rejected. In many cases, poor branding has resulted in major losses of money. That's how important your brand becomes.

Good Brand Use	Not So Good Brand	Why It's Bad?
Ronald McDonald clown	Burger King creeper king	Customers didn't get hungry after being creeped out.
Geico's gecko	Esurance's Erin girl	Fan spoofs of the company's cartoon Erin had become more racy than they wanted.
Oprah talkshow host	Geraldo talkshow host	Yeah, if you can't recall a flicker of memory about Geraldo's show, I've made my point.
HP Pavillion PC or All-in-One PC	Panasonic PCs	Panasonic used the familiar character, Woody Woodpecker as their mascot, and then promptly named their computer "The Woody" with its touch screen feature "Touch Woody" and it's browsing utility, "The Internet Pecker."

During the development stage of branding, there are two

schools of thought. If you are a growing top line business that has seen high six figures into the multi-million dollar revenue structure, you should be ready for the next step. However, high producing companies are growing and most likely have lots of moving parts making their ability to pause on this topic more difficult. It may be time to interview for a brand or marketing contractor over hiring a full time member. This is common practice. Hiring a brander may be a six to nine month project. After that a rebrand would occur as needed or branding a new product lines or service. Another way is hiring a marketing contractor. This relationship might be a year to year contract or until you reach the range of 10 or twenty million dollars. They would have other clients too, but this would allow a qualified marketer to oversee a whole vision, and from there divide and conquer several parts of your marketing areas which would include the rebrand. Tending to bringing in this role is vital to your bottom line. What if I told you a good brand design or redesign could actually capture more revenue? It's true. Imagine increasing your bottom line by simply redesigning or upgrading your brand. Allowing a branding expert in via a contract is a strategy smaller businesses fail to recognize. Even better, a marketing expert would not only be able to oversee the rebrand, but they can also recommend products, services, or propose a way to enhance your current offerings. It is definitely possible, but ask what skills the company or project needs before shopping for the right person. For example, what personality style does the project need? What controls must I keep in place, what innovation am I open to? What skills would help the company increase revenue by 20 percent? Am I prepared as an owner to allow someone else to guide, change, or infuse, and/or apply a new school of thought?

The other school of thought focuses on a small business starting out, a business making 10 to 30 thousand per month, or the business that has what I call the on-demand budget. That means you afford what seems important at the moment and the business owner does the rest. Not the wisest method to hanging a shingle, but most business owners begin that way so don't shame yourself if this is you. Take hold of it and grow into being more stable. This second group of businesses need to focus on being more clever than costly. It can happen, but it needs studiousness and awareness. Being discerning is important at this stage. I remember early in my career I had a new service that had not been on the market yet. I was so excited because we had money in the bank, which helped me relax, and like many young companies, it feels a little powerful. Cruising along, in under a year, our website was capturing 10,000 unique hits per month, there were a slew of emails coming through, and we had clients. Back in 1990s, 10,000 unique visitors to a website was outstanding. Then, along comes a valuation company. Those are companies that look at all aspects of an organization, and a logical value on what the company is worth is decided. Valuations are used to present to future investors in hopes of garnering chunks of money to use in the business. This idea was presented by a younger counterpart with a business degree. He was in the thick of business and I followed shiny round things and slick talkers at the time. I was convinced in order to gain more investors a valuation would be necessary. I did not ask logical questions like where will I find potential investors outside what they offered, what will I do if nothing happens with this, or what will I have besides knowing how much I'm worth? If I had, I may have learned when someone is ready to invest, they will want to do their own due diligence and most likely get their own valuation. If I had slowed down a bit, I also would have realized I could purchase a valuation if the need was presented. At the end, it did not add money to the bottom line. Avoiding the shiny round things and banning every slick talker is a top three action items for this level of business.

The formula for young companies is to use their time wisely with a system of related marketing pieces. In tandem, peruse other brands, dig deep and find your creative quan, and then create a few clever yet consistent pieces. This collection can be used by seasoned companies as well. They can use it to recreate some fun pieces, or revitalize a more traditional method of communication pieces. Using these together can create a brand and it would speak across collateral like websites, in specific printed pieces, on printed trinkets that get handed out, throw aways, or for fun. This also addresses the fun piece of what many young companies seek. Let's begin with the first part of the formula, an equation of decisions before developing the marketing pieces.

- Choose three colors that will be used consistently across the marketing collateral.
- Choose two complimenting font types. Use one for the large headers or titles, and the other font for the content area. The first font may have more personality and the second font will be simple and easy to read.
- Use a logo or an icon of some kind. You can move the icon or logo around. It can be larger or smaller, and it can be seen in whole, in part, as a watermark, or it can be consistently used, but use it throughout your marketing pieces.
- Keep in mind that sometimes less is more. Avoid doing all the logo ideas on one item. The most important thing is to make the reader read it, so be clever.

This is an equation to get beginners started. However, in real life, a brander or a designer works with a marketer to create materials. If you are looking for a brander or designer, look for someone from the corporate arena who has worked with high level brands, or look for a designer with a degree in fine art, design, or website design. Be careful you don't get caught in they cyclone of seeing one piece and assuming all their pieces come out consistently that way. It could be a one hit wonder. If you have not used a real designer to organize your materials, you are losing the battle before you have a real shot. At the very least you're leaving money on the table. Yes, I have seen people be successful with barely decent marketing material, but if you look closely, it will be due to another reason that has little to do with the designed material. Being great at sales can soothe the sting of poor marketing materials. Knowing how to communicate benefits easily enough for buyers to understand is another. Content that overshadows the public marketing image, or a combination of these and others helps bypass poor marketing collateral. There is a reason shabby marketing material works, but it won't be the great brand creation.

The second part of this formula are the marketing pieces. Again, a start up can use these as their first set of collateral, and an established company can use this as new innovative rebrand or enhance what they have. Here are pieces that work:

- Create a top 10 list of myths about what you do (this becomes a single card brochure).
- Create a top 10 list about jargon used in your industry with their definitions (this becomes a tip sheet when they need your service).
- Create a top 10 list of questions people ask, and then provide the answer (this becomes your FAQs).
- Create a top 10 list of your annoying habits or habits each team member is known for - in fun (this becomes the about me, about the owner, or about the team page on a website after the bios).
- Create a top 10 list of biggest challenges the company has helped clients overcome (this becomes the business success stories - your selling sheet).
- Create a top 10 list biggest problems you solve (this becomes a selling sheet).
- Create a top 10 list of what makes your company different (this becomes a useful sheet to help potential customers make a decision).

These are the basics equations that will get any business headed toward a consistent, clever brand. However, when a company is ready for their next step, the step where branding impacts the bottom line, figuring out the right brander or marketer to contract comes through the questions you ask them. Building a brand comes with unique focuses on the why and the culture and builds from there. When you generate a couple million dollars in revenue, it is time to consider a rebrand for the purpose of increasing your bottom line and expanding the business reach (aka attracting more clients). Top line brand designers can cost a small business about 50 thousand dollars, and they will be worth every penny. If a company asks for this kind of money, do not assume they are experts. The formula for choosing an excellent brand creator happens with excellent questions asked. That is the formula. This is an investment so questions like these should be included:

- How much and what kind of research do they do? Can they describe it?
- What projects have they re/designed and what are the results?
- What was their role in design previous to this role?
- What kinds of marketing collateral will they provide in the end? For example, will they provide collateral that will be translated across all mobile platforms, website headers, Facebook or LinkedIn headers, or letterhead and envelope design?
- Will they be providing high resolution jpg and png files of all the pictures used? Will they provide a Style Sheet showing the colors in Pantone, CMYK, RGB, and Hex codes?
- Will I own all the marketing creations and will you provide all the commercial files like the working Illustrator or Photoshop files?
- Will they make suggestions on expansion ideas, a kind of future look of the new brand?
- Ask for samples of their work.
- Referrals or testimonials.

The companies I recommend are Re Perez of Branding For The People. He comes from corporate and began moving brands for small business. He has several line offers including a top line services with bells and whistles, a type of DIY branding program for a few thousand dollars, and even a brand analysis for under a thousand. Another is Brands by Ovo in Portland, Oregon. They are a group of top line brand specialists that not only provide their service but educate along the way. They offer a pretty nice website with a learning component that includes brand vocabulary, brand focuses, and case studies.

If you want to learn some design know-how make a visit to Before and After Magazine. They are hard core designers. Not only that, but their marque is educating other designers and sharing their information with anyone. They offer tutorials that go beyond the outer limits with DVDs, detailed PDF tutorials, and online videos that illustrate comparisons between design samples. They are an education in what to expect from design in every aspect. This is your knowledge base. A great investment of time and money.

Whew! A sufficient amount of information in a small space is a challenge, but these formulas will get you rolling. Keep in mind this is such a massive category so expect to be evolving. New elements will enter as you grow; what is fresh today could be outdated tomorrow. However, the final piece is you. Where are you in this equation. Here are a few questions to begin shaping what you want in marketing:

1. If I were choosing adjectives, what is the overall feelings I want people to feel when they meet my company through marketing material only?

_____

_____

2. Am I willing to hear the truth about how a brander or marketer sees me today and how they see me in the future?

_____

_____

3. Am I willing to welcome a new creativity into my business?

_____

_____

Amazing
how we can light tomorrow
with today.
Elizabeth Barrett Browning

7 MAKING TIME AT HOME

The chapter title makes me giggle because depending on your age, this might mean something a little different from the actual topic of time management. So get your head back in the game and let's look at the problem. Any time you begin to multiply business into more business, you run into the proverbial problem, is there enough time for everything? You recoil at the idea of juggling family, companion, a social life, church, community, and yes, business It's a universal excuse. Ahhh, you expected me to say 'problem' but it's a management issue that society commonly excuses as a problem. It still looks like a problem, but if you really want to solve the puzzle, let's see if we can sort things out in bite sized chunks instead.

You're reading a book from a business owner who is married to a beautiful man...with a head injury. He was injured more than 20 years ago and I reared a family with seven children quasi-solo. In addition, we would welcome individuals who were down on their luck and were trying to sort things out or get back on their feet. I contributed time to church, civic groups, and community. I managed the court cases, the medical cases, the children, and worked a full time job. When I wasn't working for someone else, I owned my own business, and I have done that more than 15 years now. I was organized, there were daily chores, and the home was cleaned daily. There was homework, sports, and in-home summer school. I don't share this to make it sound like smooth sailing. On the contrary, it was everything but smooth. There were wildly crazy times. Think about it, seven children and an injury; need I say more? One meal alone meant two five foot tables pushed together, with 10 chairs, two very large casserole dishes packed with starch and protein, two dozen rolls, a quarter pound of butter, two large boxes of jello and two large cans of fruit, a green salad using a head and a half of lettuce, three gallons of water, and a pleading prayer that this would be enough for ten hungry bodies. It was the best my money, time, and sanity could do. So going back to the beginning. What is the formula for growing a business and fulfilling all the other equally important time grabbing activities? It's time in bite sized chunks.

Here are three equations that will not go wrong. Make time every week for you, your companion and the family; in that order. Do not waiver, and do not try and be the exception saying that something else prevents you from it. There is no barrier too great to prevent you from accomplishing these equations: not travel, time intense conferences, training, performing, driving, investors, mergers, appointments, no computer or phone, nothing can get inside these pieces. It may require forethought and planning for more difficult times, but it can be done.

You. It's an overlooked equation, one that lands people in burnout and depression. Among all the formulas, pieces, equations, adding, subtracting, carrying, dividing, and multiplying, this is probably the single most important piece to the whole book. Be good to you. It is obvious that the core success in business stems from your attitudes, mental toughness, feelings, alertness, accomplishments, planning, endurance, purpose, drive, and basically everything within. So it makes profound sense to take care of the heart, mind, body, soul, and overall well being of you. Do not abuse the equation, but use it. Dena had a large family; however, she always found time for herself. I thought looking good was reserved for time with her friends, which it was. But one day I stayed at her home before meeting up with friends the next day. The friends I would be connecting with were pretty outdoorsy and were known to enjoy life dressed in sweats or shorts, with hair in a ponytail, and without makeup. That means no primping, hair spray, or mousse. The next morning she and I got up to get ready. I skipped a couple steps in my makeup and hair routine, and my friend asked, "Why aren't you putting on all your makeup?" I replied that I didn't want to make my friends uncomfortable because they would not be dressed up. She replied, "I would never do that. I get dressed up for me, and I would never dress down for fear of making friends uncomfortable." While some may feel she is selfish, I counter that being focused on what feels good and healthy for you creates a healthier society. In the smallest sense I passed on doing something I liked just in case my friends were uncomfortable. Friends should not be uncomfortable with you being you. Most likely that was my issue and not theirs. That is the formula of self care. Once a week take care of you. It does not need to be a whole day, but it can be writing in a journal, getting a massage, or working on a craft. I have a friend, Connie, who is the President of a credit union. She likes to play poker, Texas Holdem, once a month with friends. She said it helps her forget about everything else and allows her to relax. This is also a great time to read scriptures, meditate, or write in a gratitude journal. Get creative, think about what moves you or will help you maintain a wholesome steadiness in your life. This is the first equation in the three pronged formula.

The second equation is caring for your companion. For many years before my husband, Don's, accidents, he worked in Hollywood, which was about two hours away from home. He would leave at 4 a.m. each morning. In addition, he played basketball three times per week, and he was the President over our men's youth group. If there were no church obligations he would come home between 8 p.m. and 11 p.m. If he was needed elsewhere, he would arrive home just in time to attend those meetings. We agreed every week we would make time with each other. One occasion I was feeling pretty drained and I was several months pregnant. That evening, about 10:30 p.m., I was talking with a young lady who was living with us at the time. We were working through some of her problems. Don walked in. We exchanged greetings between the front door and the dining room table. I knew he was heading upstairs to get cleaned up and into his pajamas. I was happy he was home but exhausted. He must have sensed it. He disappeared upstairs only to descend the staircase wearing a pair of black slacks, a pink tuxedo shirt, and a black bow tie. My mouth dropped open and everything stopped in the room. The young lady and I moved like a slow motion movie as I began to rise in my chair. He slipped around the corner into the kitchen and emerged with a picnic basket in one hand and took my hand in the other. He drove me to a church parking lot just around the corner from our home, lit a candle, and got down on one knee in our mini van. He shared his love and appreciation of my work in the home and spent the time asking me about my day. Wow! That was enough for me! That single 45 minutes gave me enough energy for months. Another idea if you are unable to be home is to send flowers with a special note, edible arrangements, or write a 'favorite songs about us' list. A variation is to put one song in a sealed envelope for each day (or every other day) of absence. Include a single line or two of the reason for that song choice. It will give you tons of mileage and remind both of you of the reasons you are building a business. Relationships need rejuvenation desperately. It needs regular reminders that building a business takes a backseat to the purpose of the relationship. Use those tender times to focus on the great things about each other. Focus on talents, interesting questions, new learning ahas, and celebrations.

When it comes to children, it is a challenge. If you listen to the "experts" you'll need to give each child 30-minutes of their own every day. For me, that would have been about four hours per day. Then there was meal making, homework, chores, church, my business, and civic activities etc. That's near impossible and heaven forbid if one of the children had needs, which happened daily. Do we cut others off? Should I guilt my way into depression? No. What can be done is cluster or chunk time. Spending focused, quality time goes a long way. There are times during a day to capture moments. Like making meals, cleaning up, going grocery shopping, helping with homework, sitting down at dinner, and just before bed. A real power tool is to take 45 minutes to an hour, one day per week of undivided attention to the family as a whole. In our home, we planned an "evening." It included a couple of items from a list. The list included crafts, talking on a topic, singing, puppets, asking and answering questions, playing a game, cooking a dessert, going somewhere, reading together, or anything the family could do together. Each person would take turns being in charge, choosing from the list, and leading the meeting. This is where conversations deepened, general well being could be gauged, leadership was developed, and bonding definitely occurred. There is no definition of a perfect scenario, and it's even more liquid when the family is young, but we did it every week without fail. It's been more than 30 years now. The children are adults and when they come over, if it's a certain day of the week, we still have that evening. Another tool to use with children is to see what skills they have that can be incorporated into the business. If they are young and can count, can they count packages or sheets of paper? Can they organize or sort? If they are gaining young man muscles, can they do lifting or loading? Can they run fliers or pack boxes? Find ways to work with them where possible. This can do a great deal to create validation, work ethic, and help children understand what the business does for the family. Finally, if you travel a bit, plan ahead and make a call home during the meeting time. Keep the children up for one very special evening if needed. In our home, my husband would spend about 10 dollars each trip to bring home "treats," which were things like shampoo from the hotel stay, a sweet from the area, a collection of cards, or some other trinket in the airport. Super easy to do when you stop for gas or after you get checked in for a flight.

If you are confused, the simple way to look at this is, make time in your life for yourself, your companion, and your family. The business life works more smoothly when the support system is cared for. If you have other activities see how much can be taken care of during work hours, and if you find yourself under water, forfeit what is the least important. To get you focused ask yourself the following questions:

1. The one thing I could do for myself each week that would relax me is…?

   _____

   _____

2. Something I could do for my companion to strengthen our commitment to each other is…?

   _____

   _____

3. An activity I would like to do with my family would be…?

   _____

The only way to do great work
is to love what you do.
If you haven't found it yet,
keep looking.
Don't settle.
Steve Jobs

8 THE SECRET SAUCE, UBER SUCCESS

To understand the power of this formula, think of it this way. The secret sauce is like the Kentucky Fried Chicken recipe. Behind the historic and succulent taste are the unknown 11 herbs and spices. Even more than a selling point, according to Raymond Allen, the man who opened the United Kingdom franchises when the Colonel opened in the U.S., the recipe is quite lengthy, beyond 11 herbs and spices. Perhaps its recipe length goes beyond measuring amounts. Perhaps it is a method of blending or how one or two of the herbs are prepared beforehand. It's a secret yet powerful sauce. I remember in my childhood days of poverty; it seems everyone has one; I was taught to put a blend of ketchup and mayonnaise on my rice. Today it is known as fry sauce; another blend that, had my family bottled it, may have made them a fortune. Another example is how to use herbs. When squeezed, pureed, warmed, or added to an oil it becomes a blend and is marketed as an essential oil that can lasso a wart or eliminate bathroom odors. In early days, pioneers used peppermint on the wood pane of their makeshift windows to keep spiders out. It was a common and edible treat, but somehow used differently, and it becomes a secret potion. How you blend, prepare, present, organize, arrange, or sell is a secret sauce, and to really launch yourself both personally and then professionally, there is a special mix of ingredients that create the formula of uber success.

To launch yourself into the stratosphere, become a speaker. I don't mean attend networking meetings to speak and I don't mean tell people you speak because you've trained at several mandatory programs. I also don't mean the self-proclaimed speaker whose friends said they're great at speaking. What I mean is the secret blend of questions, interactive activities, accountability rigors, public image training, defining a universal speaking topic that endures time, training in how to market what you know, best product offers, a book outline and a book, and an ongoing promotion channel. What I mean is… get hardcore, out of this world speaker training which provides more than a single ingredient, but applies an entire intellectual system. There are programs that train speakers, programs that build book outlines, and great photographers, but the uber success, the supreme cream is so much more. It harnesses a unique blend of several pieces, infuses the bells and whistles, and blends it into a nicely flavored outcome. Nearly all business owners lack this blend. It is even true of CEOs and top tier influencers. Speaking is the act of leaving a legacy beyond the widget, and it is the path of famed success.

The National Speakers Series would be my first recommendation to accomplish an intensive and complete program. I should know because I built it. It is an inclusive program based on marketing formulas of success. It offers all the bells and whistles and guarantees you get on stage to speak on your product, service, point of view, or whatever is determined through the program. The National Speakers Series also offers an extended promotion program renewable each year. Another is the Suzanne Evans organization. She lends a powerful program of much the same structure with a strong emphasis on top line, back of the room, product offers. Use these to become more than your product or service. Use this formula to become the expert in the industry of your product or service.

Besides a full training program, there is a fundamental equation. Whether keynote, network speaking, association speaking, it doesn't matter. They are all rooted in a fundamental equation: 10 percent content, 90 percent connection. Allow me to illustrate.

How long does it take you to name a comedian, actor, or singer you like? I can think of Kevin Hart, Johnny Depp, and Taylor Swift. Want it again? Brian Regan, Angelina Jolie, and Michael Buble. That's because I connect with their stories, I connect to their role in a movie, or the lyrics they sing, sing to my heart. Now, how long does it take to name the last trainer you listened to? See! It's easier to think of someone who created a connection than someone who provided content. Kevin Hart is comedian turning humor actor. That's because people are connecting with him. They want more of him. Do you know a trainer who has a blockbuster movie? I think not. No matter how important you feel your information is, don't get lost on what's important to your audience.

While content may be king, connection is the emperor.

I train speakers. I don't mean you pay a ridiculous amount of money and you get an outline and kicked out the door. I mean I train speakers to be fiercely outstanding. It's a six month process and includes the bells and whistles. The icing on the cake: I put them on a stage where they can rekindle or launch their speaking career, and I provided extended marketing training. My speakers are exceptional, passionate, and speak to move an audience. I have seen thousands of people who say they speak and been dismayed by most.

The number one problem of speakers is they want to be a master of everything so they master nothing. When that is the case, the best reaction is to connect. When you don't have enough time to plan and practice a really powerful keynote, find a connection. I watch it all the time. People who say nothing but people feel they know them. It takes a year or so for people to find out the person hasn't given them anything. However, for true speakers, the goal is the same.

Speakers who practice their craft, drive to make a living at it, and want to share will have connection in their plan. Spend the majority of your planning on how you will create connection. What story will illustrate your point best? Does it connect to this audience specifically? One or two tools or tips with gritty, gutsy, connection with your audience and they will say yes to learning more.

Use these few questions to prepare:

1. The one thing my product or service would do to make my customers' lives easier is…

_____

_____

2. The story that makes me know that is when…

_____

_____

3. It makes my customer's life easier because…

_____

_____

It is our darkest moments
that we must focus on the light.
Aristotle Onassis

9 SELF MOTIVATION

There are a mountain of studies that talk about motivation: intrinsic, extrinsic, incentives, commission, survival, and so on. Although the logical among us may think it unnecessary, it is absolutely needed. As a small business owner, life and business "stuff" can bog us down. When it does, you are alone. It's not something we intentionally seek out, but ick and negative thoughts chase us. It happens in the quiet times, the early morning hours, and when we allow idle mental time. People are mean and #*()@% will happen. Our partners may be less than supportive. Our children will have poor timing. Business partners let us down. Friendships are false. Customers have a limited view. The world has a crisis. Government makes poor decisions. Food tastes bad. Service is poor. Drivers cannot drive. The dog dug up the yard. Is this sounding familiar. Stuff happens and small business owners need an island to retreat to. Here is a hearty collection of quotes intended to motivate the owner. Use it daily, weekly, ponder one before going to bed, share one each morning with the children, or do what works for you. Enjoy.

"The two most important days in your life are the day you are born and the day you find out why" - Mark Twain

"On the topic of making a decision, ask yourself, does it make you feel better or do better?" -Karleen Andresen

"Amazing how we can light tomorrow with today." -Elizabeth Barrett Browning

"Nothing that you plan is going to work out. Everything is going to be totally different than the way you expected. And things will constantly challenge you. Wherever you look the world is not as solid it seems to be." -Eckhart Tolle

"The best way out is always through." -Robert Frost

"It is our darkest moments that we must focus on the light." - Aristotle Onassis

"Challenges are what make life interesting and overcoming them is what makes life meaningful." -Joshua J. Marine

"In order to succeed, your desire for success should be greater than your fear of failure." -Bill Cosby

"Happiness cannot be traveled to, owned, earned, or worn. It is the spiritual experience of living every minute with love, grace and gratitude." -Denis Waitley

"The only way to do great work is to love what you do. If you haven't found it yet, keep looking. Don't settle." -Steve Jobs

"Do not pray for an easy life, pray for the strength to endure a difficult one." -Bruce Lee

"In the depth of winter, I finally learned that within me there lay an invincible summer." -Albert Camus

"I've missed more than 9,000 shots in my career. I've lost almost 300 games. 26 times I've been trusted to take the game winning shot and missed. I've failed over and over and over again in my life. And that is why I succeed." -Michael Jordan

"Great spirits have always encountered violent opposition from mediocre minds." -Albert Einstein

"Courage is doing what you're afraid to do. There can be no courage unless you're scared." -Eddie Rickenbacker

"Accept responsibility for your life. Know that it is you who will get you where you want to go, no one else." -Les Brown

"Leadership is a potent combination of strategy and character. But if you must be without one, be without the strategy." -Norman Schwarzkopf

"Motivation is the art of getting people to do what you want them to do because they want to do it." -Dwight D. Eisenhower

"The important thing is not being afraid to take a chance. Remember, the greatest failure is to not try. Once you find something you love to do, be the best at doing it." -Debbie Fields

"Nobody ever wrote down a plan to be broke, fat, lazy, or stupid. Those things are what happen when you don't have a plan." –Larry Winget

"We are what we repeatedly do. Excellence, therefore, is not an act but a habit." -Aristotle

"What you get by achieving your goals is not as important as what you become by achieving your goals." -Goethe

"Desire is the starting point of all achievement, not a hope, not a wish, but a keen pulsating desire which transcends everything." -Napoleon Hill

"Remember that happiness is a way of travel, not a destination." -Roy Goodman

"When I hear somebody say, 'Life is hard,' I am always tempted to ask, 'Compared to what?'" - Sydney J. Harris

"I don't focus on what I'm up against. I focus on my goals and I try to ignore the rest." -Venus Williams

"Many of life's failures are people who did not realize how close they were to success when they gave up." -Thomas Edison

"Pain nourishes courage." -Mary Tyler Moore

"Whenever you find yourself on the side of the majority, it's time to pause and reflect."-Mark Twain

"I have never let my schooling interfere with my education." -Mark Twain

"Motivation is a fire from within. If someone else tries to light that fire under you, chances are it will burn very briefly." -Stephen Covey

"The thing that got me over the hump was accepting that I had to do whatever I could to stay in the game" -Dennis Eckersley

"There is no bag limit on happiness" -Ted Nugent

"The most valuable thing you can make is a mistake – you can't learn anything from being perfect." -Adam Osborne

"Learn to say 'no' to the good so you can say 'yes' to the best." -John C Maxwell

"What would you do if you knew you could not fail?" -Robert H Schuller

"Never, Never, Never Give up." -Winston Churchill

"I have not failed. I've just found 10,000 ways that won't work." -Thomas Edison

"Failure defeats losers, failure inspires winners." -Robert T. Kiyosaki

"Start a business while you are young. You have few commitments and are used to living off Ramen Noodles." -Dr. Sebora

"Follow your passion, not your paycheck.. The money will come eventually." -Unknown

"Ambition is the path to success. Persistence is the vehicle you arrive in." Bill Bradley

"How many people are completely successful in every department of life? Not one. The most successful people are the ones who learn from their mistakes and turn their failures into opportunities." -Zig Ziglar

"I can accept failure, everyone fails at something. But I cannot accept not trying." -Michael Jordan

"In every success story, you will find someone who has made a courageous decision." -Peter F. Drucker

"If you can dream it, you can do it." -Walt Disney

"A man who wakes up and finds himself a success hasn't been asleep." -Dave Thomas

"Continuous learning is the minimum requirement for success in any field." -Dennis Waitley

"Everyone who achieves success in a great venture solves each problem as they came. They helped themselves and they were helped through powers known and unknown to them at the time they set out on their voyage. They keep going regardless of the obstacles they meet." -W. Clement Stone

"Behind every adversity is an opportunity. If you lament over the adversity, you will miss the opportunity." -Ajaero Tony Martins

"Yet a little sleep, a little slumber and a little folding of hands to sleep; so shall your poverty come." -Proverbs 6: 10-11

18. "See thou a man diligent in his business? He shall stand before kings; he shall not stand before vain men." -Proverbs 22: 29

19. "Experience taught me a few things. One is to listen to your gut no matter how good something sounds on paper. The second is that you are generally better off sticking with what you know and the third is that sometimes, your best investments are the ones you don't make." -Donald Trump

"If you hear a voice within you saying 'you are not a painter' then by all means paint and that voice will be silenced." -Vincent Van Gogh

"Before honor is humility." -Proverbs 15: 33

"Never be ashamed! There's some who will hold it against you, but they are not worth bothering with." -J.K. Rowling

"He that observes the wind shall not sow and he that regards the clouds shall not reap." -The Holy Bible

"Singleness of purpose is essential for success in life." -John D. Rockefeller

"Embrace bad news to learn where you need the most improvement." -Bill Gates

"But thou should remember the Lord your God; for it is he that gives the power to make wealth." -Deuteronomy 8: 18

"When you reach an obstacle, turn it into an opportunity. You have the choice. You can overcome and be a winner, or you can allow it to overcome you and be a loser. The choice is yours and yours alone. Refuse to throw in the towel. Go that extra mile that failures refuse to travel. It is far better to be exhausted from success than to be rested from failure." -Mary Kay Ash

"Follow your instincts, that's where true wisdom manifest itself." -Oprah Winfrey

"All my life, people have said that I wasn't going to make it." – Ted Turner

"When I have fully decided that a result is worth getting, I go ahead of it and make trial after trial until it comes." -Ted Turner

"To win big, you sometimes have to take big risks." -Bill Gates

"Aim for the moon. If you miss it, you may hit a star." -W. Clement Stone

"Success is about creating value." -Candice Carpenter

"Good is not enough. You've got to be great." -Simon Cowell

"The energy of a mustard seed is all you need." -Karleen Andresen

"You are nuts and you should be proud of it. Stick with what you believe in." -Trip Hawkins

"I am a woman who came from the cotton fields of the South. From there I was promoted to the washtub. From there I was promoted to the cook kitchen. And from there I promoted myself into the business of manufacturing hair goods and preparations....I have built my own factory on my own ground." -Madame C. J. Walker

"Press on. Nothing in the world can take the place of persistence. Talent will not; nothing is more common than unsuccessful men with talent. Genius will not; the world is full of educated derelicts. Persistence and determination alone are omnipotent." -Ray Kroc

"Behind every small business, there's a story worth knowing. All the corner shops in our towns and cities, the restaurants, cleaners, gyms, hair salons, hardware stores – these didn't come out of nowhere." - Paul Ryan

"To be successful, you have to have your heart in your business, and your business in your heart." -Thomas Watson, Sr.

"I can't imagine a person becoming a success who doesn't give this game of life everything he's got." -Walter Cronkite

"I'm happy as long as I am making other people happy." -Dominique Ansel, Dominique Ansel Bakery

"I'm convinced that about half of what separates the successful entrepreneurs from the non-successful ones is pure perseverance." - Steve Jobs

"Those who want to lack or slack will always find a reason to support it" -Karleen Andresen

"We're a society of experiences running into each other, and we're taking it personal" -Karleen Andresen

"People want to be motivated more than they want to be educated." - Karleen Andresen

"Looking, just briefly, at the worst case scenario can prevent failure." -Karleen Andresen

"More than 75 percent of small businesses will fold within their first years, and it will be their hearts that fail them." -Karleen Andresen

"Brilliance is between the ears. Courage is between the arms." - Karleen Andresen

Thank you to the following websites: blog.FiveStars.com; BrainyQuote.com; ExaminedExistence.com; KarleenAndresen.com; MyTopBusinessIdeas.com; ThinkEntrepreneurship.com

Brilliance is between the ears
Courage is between the arms
Karleen Andresen

10 WHAT NOW?

Connect with me. If you feel moved to do so, connect with me. Using the things you read, do you feel drawn to this work? You may have only read the first paragraph of each chapter, maybe you read the last paragraph, or the table of contents, but if you feel moved to be connected, do so. If you are one of the few that read the whole book, definitely connect with me. If you feel I may be able to provide you with more insights, if you feel following me may create an positive opportunity for you, if you want a chance at something more than what you have, please feel invited. This is your moment. What did it do for you?

The quote, brilliance is between the ears and courage is between the arms is the what now moment. Brilliance are all the things you think. Some people are born churning innovation in their mind. They fall asleep with great ideas and awake with different ones. They can't help their selves. They see situations and know how to make them better. Still others have one, two, or three ideas and create impactful results and then grow them. Brilliance can be a great speech or knowing you need to walk away. It's what your mind does in the quiet moments too. That's your brilliance. Courage comes from the heart. It's between the arms. Courage from the heart also means what you embrace or let go of too. It's the feelings. How you feel about letting go of things that aren't good for you, how you feel when you embrace something outstanding. It could be the one step forward, two steps back that happens because you're embracing and letting go at the same time. You use both in business. Brilliance innovates, thinks logically, and the heart pushes you onward or pulls you back. To be a success, you need both brilliance and courage: think it, feel it, do it.

If you would like to connect with me, and I hope you do, I will provide you a free gift and keep you informed of ways you can engage in our activities.

Grab my gift for you: KarleenAndresen.com/bookgift

If something is worth doing
It's worth overdoing

11 BONUS

Someone told me, if it's worth doing, it's worth overdoing. This chapter is overdoing it. I am fitting these in for those "I want more" types. There are so many other formulas because everything is a formula in some way, shape, or form. These are to prove the point.

Escalating Intimacy Equation (great for sales too)
Immersing this equation into your life and business patterns can only enhance progress and profitability, but also provides a nice balance to ambition. Leading these questions with a non-threatening tone and body language is a plus.
- Ask permission
    - When entering into a tender topic, when wanting to get to know someone better, when in conflict, asking permission to to be invited in is an excellent approach. It depends on the situation, but there are many entry points. For example, "Can I share something on that topic….Are you open for some training at this moment….Can I take a photo of you.

...Could I schedule a meeting with you....Could I ask you a question."

- Ask 50 thousand foot questions
  - These are questions like, "At this point in your life, what would be your best piece of advice to the world...people your age...people starting out... people in your situation....What's a struggle you're dealing with right now...." It's open, broad, big idea questions.
- Respond with a question in opposite
  - This is where intimacy takes flight. In a professional setting, the bond begins to form here. If someone answers the 50 thousand foot question, "At this point in your life, what's your advice to others?" and they respond with, "Do everything yourself," your response would be, "Tell me about a time you didn't do everything yourself," or "What have you seen that makes you feel others should do everything their self?" And then listen with interest to understand.

Just for fun, this equation can rekindle a sweet side of romance. Try it the next time you're with a companion. Don't flinch at the double-takes, just go with it as if you've been doing it forever.

Breakeven Equation

Knowing how much it costs to run your business is critical because in most cases you're bootstrapping and a misstep can turn the business account upside down if a client check didn't clear. For established businesses, the same is true because you tend to turn your head and allow the animals to run the store. Too many people have lost loads of money because they trusted staff too easily. The freedom goes to their head. I used to co-own a food franchise, which is long code for we pay the franchise to use their name, their recipes, to advertise for us, and we reap the rewards of the village mentality. (Sales price x Units) - (Variable cost x Units) - Fixed costs = $

Profit Margin Formula

There are opinions all over the globe about profit margins. A profit is the amount of money you make over what how much you're paying to produce the product or service. Amazon broke the ceiling on what to expect because they were in debt for years and yet people still invested in them. Think about it. Investors were investing in a company losing money according to the graphs. Does that seem like a sound business decision? While that is a unique story, business owners should know a general rule of thumb. It happens with speakers and other service organizations. They just don't know what to charge for their product or service. There are other factors to consider; however, this serves as an excellent, basic rule of thumb: add three to five times the cost to find your selling price.

- 3 times cost

  cost to produce the product or service x 3 = selling price
- 4 times cost

  cost to produce the product or service x 4 = selling price
- 5 times cost

  cost to produce the product or service x 5 = selling price

If you're a company that sells boxes of children's crayons, then calculate how much the crayons cost to make. Count up the cost of colors, wax, box, paper wrappers around the crayons, printing, stickers, credit card processing fees, and anything else you're paying for to make that a single box of crayons. If you find out it costs $.50 to make, then to achieve a five times profit, you would charge $2.50 per box. That's $.50 x 5 = $2.50 per box. While this does not include the fixed costs like forms, manual labor, delivery, design fees, and online website fees, for a young business, this formula provides the buffer in the markup price.

If you are in the service business and your major 'product' is intelligence, then you want to consider costs like time to design overall, time to customize, cost of the time you provide in training, copies, printing, and consulting with an expert for you or the company.

Net Profit Money Model

This looks confusing, but go slow and you should be fine. The first equation is the net profit money model. The next section is showing how to work the numbers to get to the first equation. And the third is an example of the equation in action.

(Fixed Cost + Desired Profit) / (Price - Variable Cost Per Unit) = Net Revenue Model (aka: Breakeven)

Fixed Costs + Desired Profit = x
Price - Variable Cost per Unit = y
X/Y = How many units you need to sell to achieve the net profit

Fixed Cost (250) + Desired Profit (10,000) = X (10,250)
Price (1,000) - cost per unit (150) = Y (850)
X (10,250) / Y (850) = number of people enrolled (12.05)

Blog Post Formula

Ever wonder how many posts is a good rule of thumb? It takes practice to become good at blogging, and the only way to do that is to dive in. Some blogs may require a limited number of posts, but for the most part, the more engagement the better. Plan to engage if you want to gain followers or become the expert. There are other elements like creative posts and having a marquee style. If you don't have that, it will come. For companies who have others do the company posts, make sure they understand and communicate the tone and culture of the company instead of using their own voice. Many disasters have happened when this is overlooked. Another is key words and phrases you will want to learn about. Those are usually words or phrases that connect to your business, the industry, or the product or service you're selling. For now, what's important is beginning. Here's a model to use:

- 1 time per week - Forget it if you're using this for business, but family members may like this post schedule.
- 3 times per week - Now we're talking. You're kind of serious about the talking points, but don't expect to be considered serious just yet.
- 5 times per week - Yep, you've got the hang of it. You hopefully have a list of topics, perhaps themes each week, and you're keeping posts to a 300-500 word minimum (yes, some people say more, but ask what you read).
- 6 or more posts per week - King! You win! This is someone who integrates with their audience. They bring information that is interesting and varied. It can be themes, but most likely it's about the visitors. This poster is interested in having interaction, connection, and providing what is useful.

Formula of the Product Lifecycle

People think products and services are bad if they lose affinity with their audience. That may be the case, but a product's life cycle is also true. Many times small business owners go into a depression because they don't attract the sales they used to, or they a having people unsubscribe to their company offerings. Have no fear, it's important to know that every product has a life cycle. Expect it, and reinvent the company offerings if you want to stay in the game. Here it is:

Development ▶ Introduction ▶ Growth ▶ Maturity ▶ Decline

ABOUT THE AUTHOR

Karleen Andresen is a marketing coach and fierce in her pursuits to forge small business forward. She was a column writer for McClatchy Company, a leading newspapers and Internet publishing company, she publishes on LinkedIn, and has written many articles for business magazines. She speaks and trains regularly on marketing, leadership, personal development, team improvement, and conflict resolution. Karleen has a B.S. in Marketing and a M.S. in Negotiations and Conflict Resolution.

Karleen's Top 10 "I never..." Statements

I never had braces
I never wore glasses or contacts (until now)
I never ate a beet
I never danced in the rain
I never went blonde
I never partied
I never lose hope
I never stop dreaming
I never expected less
I never want us to fail

www.ingramcontent.com/pod-product-compliance
Lightning Source LLC
Chambersburg PA
CBHW071608200326
41519CB00021BB/6919